LEVEL
1
YOU READ | I READ

Susan B. Anthony

Kitson Jazynka

NATIONAL GEOGRAPHIC

Washington, D.C.

How to Use This Book

Reading together is fun! When older and younger readers share the experience, it opens the door to new learning. As you read together, talk about what you learn.

YOU READ

This side is for a parent, older sibling, or older friend. Before reading each page, take a look at the words and pictures. Talk about what you see. Point out words that might be hard for the younger reader.

I READ

This side is for the younger reader.

As you read, look for the bolded words. Talk about them before you read.

At the end of each chapter, do the activity together.

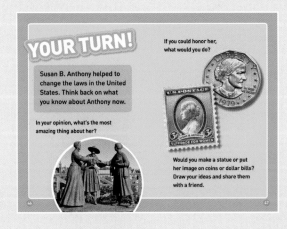

Table of Contents

VOTES FOR WOMEN

CHAPTER 1

Who Was Susan B. Anthony?

Susan B. Anthony was a woman who fought to change unfair laws. She spoke up about equal **rights**. Some say she was a superhero. But she didn't wear a cape or fly through the air. Instead, she wore a red silk shawl and a lace collar. She wore her hair in a bun.

Anthony said women should be treated the same as men. They should have the same **rights**.

a rally for women's right to vote

5

This illustration shows New York City from across the water in the 1820s.

Anthony was born about 200 years ago. The laws at that time in the United States were not fair to everyone. Not all adults in the United States were allowed to **vote**. Anthony believed that if women could vote, the laws might be fairer.

Back then, women couldn't **vote**. Anthony said that women should have that right.

Vote NO on Woman Suffrage

BECAUSE 90% of the women either do not want it, or *do not care.*

BECAUSE it means *competition* of women with men instead of *co-operation.*

BECAUSE 80% of the women eligible to vote are married and can only double or annul their husbands' votes.

BECAUSE it can be of no benefit commensurate with the additional expense involved.

BECAUSE in some States more voting women than voting men will place the Government under petticoat rule.

BECAUSE it is unwise to risk the good we already have for the evil which may occur.

Household Hints

National Association OPPOSED to Woman Suffrage

Headquarters
268 Madison Avenue
New York, N. Y.

Branch
726 Fourteenth Street, N. W.
Washington, D. C.

Votes of Women can accomplish no more than votes of Men. Why waste time, energy and money, without result?

This flyer was put out by people who thought women should not have the right to vote.

YOUR TURN!

When you vote, you tell leaders what you think. You vote in an election. You can vote for the people who make the laws. Sometimes you can vote to say whether or not you agree with a law.

Have an election with your friends and family!

1 Color three pictures.

2 Have your friends and family vote on which picture you should hang up.

3 The picture that gets the most votes wins!

CHAPTER 2

Growing Up

Susan B. Anthony was born on February 15, 1820, in Adams, Massachusetts, U.S.A. She was the second oldest of six siblings. Her **family** belonged to the Religious Society of Friends, also called Quakers. They lived a simple life. They wore plain clothing, had few belongings, and worked hard. They believed all people were equal.

the home where Susan B. Anthony was born

SUSAN B. ANTHONY BIRTHPLACE

This art shows a Quaker family on a farm.

 Anthony's **family** taught their children that it didn't matter if you were a man, a woman, black, or white.

Susan B. Anthony was born in this room. Today, the house is a museum.

Anthony's father owned a mill. Her mother ran their busy house. As a girl, Anthony helped her parents at home. She cooked, sewed, and worked in the garden. She also went to **school**.

Anthony knew **school** was important. She learned everything she could.

Children learned from books like these when Anthony was a child.

When Anthony grew up, she worked as a **teacher**. Anthony taught her students reading, writing, and math. But she earned much less money than teachers who were men.

This one-room schoolhouse, shown in about 1900, had students of all different ages. Anthony would have taught in a school like this one.

 She thought that was unfair. She thought all **teachers** should earn the same amount of money for doing the same job.

YOUR TURN!

School in the 1820s was different from how it is today. How was it different from your school?

Children often attended one-room schoolhouses.

Classes included children of many different ages.

Kids skipped school to help tend to their families' farms.

CHAPTER 3

Changing the World

YOU READ

In Anthony's time, many people were enslaved. Most Quaker families believed slavery should be **abolished** (uh-BALL-ished), or stopped.

Anthony also believed slavery should be **abolished**.

NOTICE.

THE DUTCHESS COUNTY

ANTI-SLAVERY

SOCIETY

Will hold its first Annual Meeting at the house of Stephen E. Flagler, in the village of *Pleasant Valley*,

ON THURSDAY,

The 25th inst.

☞Several gentlemen will ADDRESS the meeting.☜

A neat and spacious Room, fitted for a large audience of Ladies and Gentlemen, is provided for the occasion.

All who feel an interest in the PRESER

VATION OF THEIR LIBERTIES are respect-

fully invited to attend.

P. S. Meeting for Business at 11, A. M.—for Ad

dresses at half past 2, P. M.

April 22, 1839.

This flyer announces a meeting of an anti-slavery society.

19

In 1845, Anthony's family moved to a farm in Rochester, New York, U.S.A. Abolitionists (ab-oh-LISH-un-ists) met at the Anthony family farm on Sundays. They shared ideas. They talked about **fairness**.

the Anthony family farm in Rochester, New York, around 1850

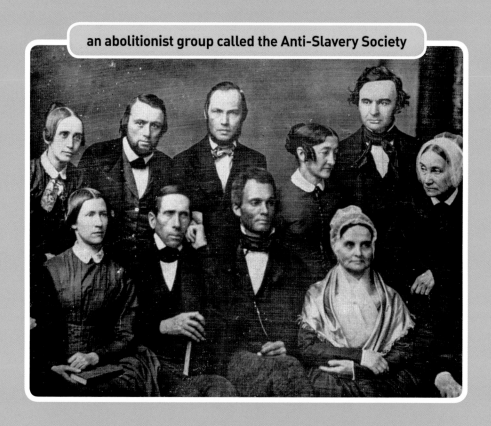

an abolitionist group called the Anti-Slavery Society

 Soon, Anthony joined her family at the farm. At the meetings, she shared her ideas about **fairness**, too. She helped write speeches.

A man named Frederick Douglass often joined the meetings. He had been a slave. He worked to convince others that everyone should have the right to vote.

Anthony listened to his speeches. She knew it was important to **speak**. In 1849, she gave a speech of her own. She talked about women's rights.

A woman speaks to a crowd about women's rights, in 1908.

Many people thought women should not **speak** in public. But Anthony used bold words. She said what she believed in.

This art shows the first African Americans to cast a legal vote in the U.S.

 In 1865, slavery ended in the United States. A few years later, U.S. leaders **changed** the law so that all adult men could vote, no matter the color of their skin.

But some things hadn't **changed.** Women still didn't have the right to vote.

This art shows men counting votes in a presidential election.

YOUR TURN!

Look at these important events in Anthony's life. Put them in the order in which they happened.

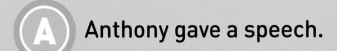 **A** Anthony gave a speech.

B Anthony became a teacher.

C Anthony moved to New York.

D Anthony was born.

ANSWER: D, Anthony was born.
B, Anthony became a teacher.
C, Anthony moved to New York.
A, Anthony gave a speech.

CHAPTER 4

Working Harder

Now that black men had the right to vote, Anthony worked even harder to give women the same right.

Women at the time were expected to be quiet and follow the rules, but Anthony shared her opinions. She also chose not to marry. Sometimes she wore pants called **bloomers**.

women working for the right to vote

Most women wore skirts.
But **bloomers** made it easier
for Anthony to do her work.

 Anthony worked with another friend who shared her **ideas**. She and Elizabeth Cady Stanton gave speeches. Together, they traveled around the United States.

Elizabeth Cady Stanton (left) and Susan B. Anthony

Anthony (in blue) and another woman come up to a stage to speak.

 Anthony and Stanton knocked on people's doors. They told the people about their **ideas**.

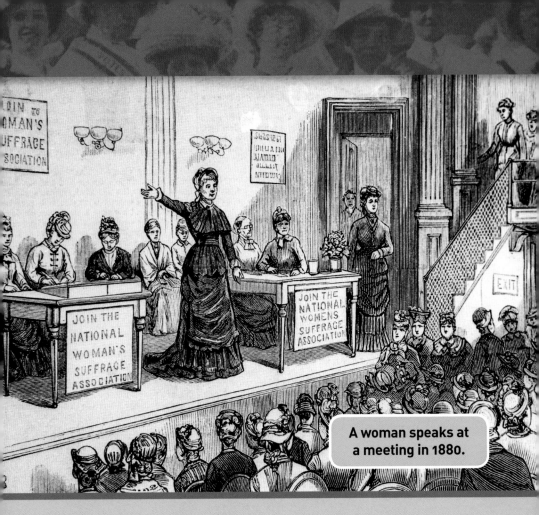

A woman speaks at a meeting in 1880.

YOU READ

All across the country, they found people who agreed with their ideas. They asked these people to sign a **petition** (peh-TIH-shun), a piece of paper that said what their ideas were. Anthony and Stanton spoke to leaders. They asked the leaders for change. Sometimes the leaders laughed. Sometimes they listened. But they didn't change the laws.

Anthony showed the leaders the **petition**. She said that people wanted the laws to change.

A PETITION
FOR
UNIVERSAL SUFFRAGE.

To the Senate and House of Representatives:

The undersigned, Women of the United States, respectfully ask an amendment of the Constitution that shall prohibit the several States from disfranchising any of their citizens on the ground of sex.

In making our demand for Suffrage, we would call your attention to the fact that we represent fifteen million people—one half the entire population of the country—intelligent, virtuous, native-born American citizens; and yet stand outside the pale of political recognition.

The Constitution classes us as "free people," and counts us *whole* persons in the basis of representation; and yet are we governed without our consent, compelled to pay taxes without appeal, and punished for violations of law without choice of judge or juror.

The experience of all ages, the Declarations of the Fathers, the Statute Laws of our own day, and the fearful revolution through which we have just passed, all prove the uncertain tenure of life, liberty and property so long as the ballot—the only weapon of self-protection—is not in the hand of every citizen.

Therefore, as you are now amending the Constitution, and, in harmony with advancing civilization, placing new safeguards round the individual rights of four millions of emancipated slaves, we ask that you extend the right of Suffrage to Woman—the only remaining class of disfranchised citizens—and thus fulfil your Constitutional obligation "to Guarantee to every State in the Union a Republican form of Government."

As all partial application of Republican principles must ever breed a complicated legislation as well as a discontented people, we would pray your Honorable Body, in order to simplify the machinery of government and ensure domestic tranquillity, that you legislate hereafter for persons, citizens, tax-payers, and not for class or caste.

For justice and equality your petitioners will ever pray.

NAMES.	RESIDENCE.
Elizabeth Stanton	New York
Susan B. Anthony	Rochester — N.Y.
Antoinette Brown Blackwell	New York
Lucy Stone	Newark, N. Jersey

In 1868, Anthony and Stanton started a **newspaper**. They called it *The Revolution.* Articles in the newspaper made people think. They also made people talk and argue about ideas.

The Revolution.

PRINCIPLE, NOT POLICY: JUSTICE, NOT FAVORS.

VOL. I.—NO. 1.

NEW YORK, WEDNESDAY, JANUARY 8, 1868.

$2.00 A YEAR.

The Revolution;

THE ORGAN OF THE

NATIONAL PARTY OF NEW AMERICA.

PRINCIPLE, NOT POLICY—INDIVIDUAL RIGHTS AND RESPONSIBILITIES.

THE REVOLUTION WILL ADVOCATE:

1. In POLITICS—Educated Suffrage, Irrespective of Sex or Color; Equal Pay to Women for Equal Work; Eight Hours Labor; Abolition of Standing Armies and Party Despotisms. Down with Politicians—Up with the People!

2. In RELIGION—Deeper Thought; Broader Ideas; Science not Superstition; Personal Purity; Love to Man as well as God.

3. In SOCIAL LIFE—Morality and Reform; Practical Education, not Theoretical; Facts not Fiction; Virtue not Vice; Cold Water not Alcoholic Drinks or Medicines. It will indulge in no Gross Personalities and Immoral Advertisements, so common in Religious Newspapers.

4. The REVOLUTION proposes a new Commercial and Financial Policy. America no longer led by Europe. Gold like our Corn for sale. Greenbacks for money. An American System of Finance. American Products and Labor Free. Foreign Manufactures Prohibited. Open doors to Artisans

KANSAS.

THE question of the enfranchisement of woman has already passed the court of moral discussion, and is now fairly ushered into the arena of politics, where it must remain a fixed element of debate, until party necessity shall compel its success.

With 9,000 votes in Kansas, one-third the entire vote, every politician must see that the friends of "woman's suffrage" hold the balance of power in that State to-day. And those 9,000 votes represent a principle deep in the hearts of the people, for this triumph was secured without money, without a press, without a party. With these instrumentalities now fast coming to us on all sides, the victory in Kansas is but the herald of greater victories in every State of the Union. Kansas already leads the world in her legislation for woman on questions of property, education, wages, marriage and divorce. Her best universities are open alike to boys and girls. In fact woman has a voice in the legislation of that State. She votes on all school questions and is eligible to the office of trustee. She has a voice in temperance too; no license is granted without the consent of a majority of the adult citizens, male and female, black and white. The consequence is, stone school houses are voted up in every part of the State, and rum voted down. Many of the ablest men in that State are champions of woman's cause. Governors, judges, lawyers and clergymen. Two-thirds of the press and pulpits advocate the idea.

ence outside as well as inside the State, all combined might have made our vote comparatively a small one, had not George Francis Train gone into the State two weeks before the election and galvanized the Democrats into their duty, thus securing 9,000 votes for woman's suffrage. Some claim that we are indebted to the Republicans for this vote; but the fact that the most radical republican district, Douglass County, gave the largest vote against woman's suffrage, while Leavenworth, the Democratic district, gave the largest vote for it, fully settles that question.

In saying that Mr. Train helped to swell our vote takes nothing from the credit due all those who labored faithfully for months in that State. All praise to Olympia Brown, Lucy Stone, Susan B. Anthony, Henry B. Blackwell, and Judge Wood, who welcomed, for an idea, the hardships of travelling in a new State, fording streams, scaling rocky brinks, sleeping on the ground and eating hard tack, with the fatigue of constant speaking, in school-houses, barns, mills, depots and the open air; and especially, all praise to the glorious Hutchinson family—John, his son Henry and daughter, Viola—who, with their own horses and carriage, made the entire circuit of the state, singing Woman's Suffrage into souls that logic could never penetrate. Having shared with them the hardships, with them I rejoice in our success.

E. C. S.

THE BALLOT

Members of a group against women's voting rights tear up a banner that supports equal rights.

 Some people didn't like Anthony's **newspaper**. They ripped it up.

YOU READ Many people didn't want change.
They said mean things to Anthony.
But Anthony didn't let unkind words
stop her. She wrote even more
articles and books.

HEADQUARTE
OPPOS
WOMAN S

WA

Anthony used **articles** and books to tell people about equal rights. She kept trying.

YOUR TURN!

Susan B. Anthony and Elizabeth Cady Stanton believed women should have the right to vote. They wanted to convince others to believe it, too. Some people disagreed with their ideas. Other people didn't know about their ideas.

How did Anthony and Stanton share their ideas with people?

Talk with a friend or family member about something you believe in.

How can you share your ideas with people?

CHAPTER 5

Failure Is Impossible

Anthony believed she had a right to vote, just like white men and then black men.

There was an election in 1872 to choose a president. Anthony went to the voting place and cast her vote. Two weeks later, she was **arrested** for voting.

This art from a newspaper in 1870 shows women trying to vote.

Because she was **arrested**, Anthony had to pay a $100 fine. Anthony said she would not pay.

A crowd watches a police officer arresting women who were protesting for the right to vote.

"NO SELF RESPECTING WOMAN SHOULD WISH OR WORK FOR THE SUCCESS OF A PARTY THAT IGNORES HER S[...]." SUSAN B. ANTHONY 1872

 YOU READ

Anthony kept working. Others kept working, too. Slowly, **laws** began to change. Now, women could own property and control their own money.

Laws were more fair for women now. But they still couldn't vote.

In 1906, Anthony gave a speech at her 86th birthday party. She said, "Failure is **impossible**." The same year, she died at her home in Rochester, New York.

In 1920, women finally won the right to vote. In the next election, more than eight million American women voted for the first time.

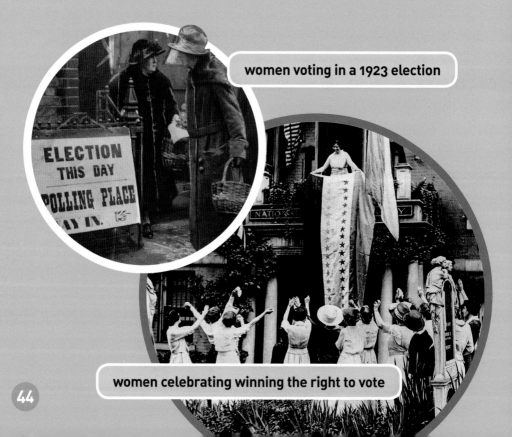

women voting in a 1923 election

women celebrating winning the right to vote

 Anthony had been right. Her dream was not **impossible**.

YOUR TURN!

Susan B. Anthony helped to change the laws in the United States. Think back on what you know about Anthony now.

In your opinion, what's the most amazing thing about her?

If you could honor her,
what would you do?

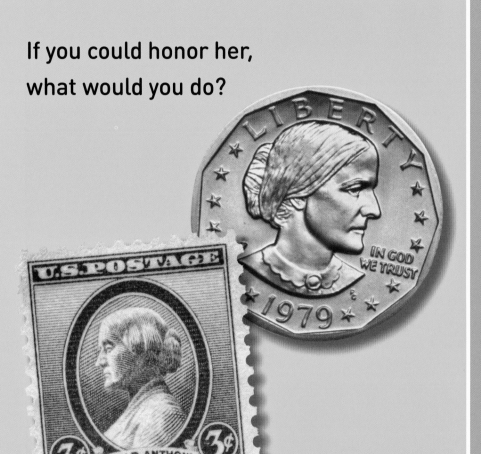

Would you make a statue or put
her image on coins or dollar bills?
Draw your ideas and share them
with a friend.

For Quinn and Aidan —K.J.

Designed by YAY! Design

The author and publisher gratefully acknowledge the expert content review by Linda Lopata, director of Interpretation and Guest Services, the National Susan B. Anthony Museum and House, and the expert literacy review by Kimberly Gillow, principal, Chelsea School District, Michigan.

Photo Credits

ASP=Alamy Stock Photo; BI=Bridgeman Images; BM/GI=Bettmann/Getty Images; GI=Getty Images; LOC=Library of Congress; SS=Shutterstock

Cover: (foreground), Everett Collection Inc/ASP; (background), Everett Historical/SS; top border (throughout), North Wind Picture Archives/ASP; 1, PhotoQuest/GI; 3, Ken Florey Suffrage Collection/Gado/GI; 4, Cindy Miller Hopkins/Danita Delimont/ASP; 5, BM/GI; 6, Interim Archives/GI; 7, History and Art Collection/ASP; 8 (LE), Leo L., age 8; 8 (RT), Elsie S., age 9; 9 (UP), sergijn/SS; 9 (LO), Kaya D., age 12; 10, Lee Snider Photo Images/SS; 11, unidentified American rural scene with Quaker family, English School, (20th century)/Private Collection/© Look and Learn/BI; 12, Courtesy of the Susan B. Anthony Birthplace Museum; 13 (LE), INTERFOTO/ASP; 13 (RT), BM/GI; 14–15, One Room School (b/w photo)/Underwood Archives/UIG/BI; 16, Old Paper Studios/ASP; 17 (UP), Old Paper Studios/ASP; 17 (LO), "In the Farmyard," (oil on canvas), Dupre, Julien (1851–1910)/Private Collection/Photo © Christie's Images/BI; 18, Album/Art Resource, NY; 19, Lanmas/ASP; 20, Courtesy of the National Susan B. Anthony Museum and House; 21, Anti-Slavery Society, including Lucretia Mott (b/w photo), American Photographer, (19th century)/Schlesinger Library, Radcliffe Institute, Harvard University/BI; 22, BM/GI; 23, Museum of London/Heritage Images/GI; 24, "The First Vote," pub. Harpers Weekly, 1867 (engraving), Waud, Alfred Rudolph (1828–91)/Private Collection/The Stapleton Collection/BI; 25, Universal History Archive/Universal Images Group via GI; 26, C.M. Bell/LOC Prints and Photographs Division; 27 (UP LE), Aquir/SS; 27 (UP RT), Paul Brady/ASP; 27 (LO), Bill Oxford/GI; 28, Everett Collection, Inc.; 29, LOC/Corbis/VCG via GI; 30, BM/GI; 31, North Wind Picture Archives/ASP; 32, BM/GI; 33, Smith Collection/Gado/ASP; 34, LOC Prints and Photographs Division; 35, Topical Press Agency/GI; 36–37, Harris & Ewing/LOC Prints and Photographs Division; 38, LOC/Corbis/VCG via GI; 39 (UP), FatCamera/GI; 39 (LO), Andy Gibson/ASP; 40, Everett Collection Historical/ASP; 41, LOC/Corbis/VCG via GI; 42, Universal History Archive/Universal Images Group via GI; 43 (UP), Ken Florey Suffrage Collection/Gado/GI; 43 (LO), History Collection 2016/ASP; 44 (LE), Popperfoto/GI; 44 (RT), World History Archive/ASP; 45, World History Archive/ASP; 46, Ilene MacDonald/ASP; 47 (LE), Michael Seleznev/ASP; 47 (RT), Time Life Pictures/Timepix/The LIFE Images Collection via GI

Library of Congress Cataloging-in-Publication Data
Names: Jazynka, Kitson, author.
Title: National geographic readers : Susan B. Anthony / by Kitson Jazynka.
Other titles: Susan B. Anthony
Description: Washington, DC : National Geographic Kids, 2019. | Series: National geographic readers | Audience: Ages 4-6 | Audience: Grades K-1
Identifiers: LCCN 2019034700 (print) | LCCN 2019034701 (ebook) | ISBN 9781426335082 (paperback) | ISBN 9781426335099 (library binding) | ISBN 9781426335105 (ebook)
Subjects: LCSH: Anthony, Susan B. (Susan Brownell), 1820-1906--Juvenile literature. | Feminists--United States--Biography--Juvenile literature. | Suffragists--United States--Biography--Juvenile literature. | Women, White--Suffrage--United States--History--Juvenile literature. | Feminism--United States--History--Juvenile literature.
Classification: LCC HQ1413.A55 J39 2019 (print) | LCC HQ1413.A55 (ebook) | DDC 305.42092 [B]--dc23
LC record available at https://lccn.loc.gov/2019034700
LC ebook record available at https://lccn.loc.gov/2019034701

National Geographic supports K–12 educators with ELA Common Core Resources.
Visit natgeoed.org/commoncore for more information.

Printed in the United States of America
19/WOR/1